The Art of Remaining Practical Foundations

~

Unlocking Your Growth & Success with Emotional Intelligence

Copyright © 2021 by Samella England.
Illustrations copyright © 2021 by Samella England
All Rights Reserved.
No part of this book may be reproduced, stored in a retrieval system, utilized or transmitted in any
form by any means, electronic or mechanical, including photocopying, recording or any information
without the written permission of the author. Inquiries should be sent to:

Msz. England
7918 El Cajon Blvd #N355
La Mesa, CA 91942
Designed and Produced By:
Samella England and We Are Our Ancestors Keeper's
Published By: We Are Our Ancestors Keeper's
Photographers: DJ DOC ReviveOurCulture &
Raymond Williams (GYM Lifestyle LLC)

The Art of Remaining

~

Practical Foundations for the Cultural and Heritage of Colored Women

Darkness Cannot Drive Out Darkness; Only Light Can Do That

⠀⠀⠀⠀⠀⠀⠀⠀⠀⠀Dr. Martin Luther King Jr.

This Book is Dedicated to:

Mama Carla Mason who helped with the delivery of my 1st born

&

My Business Dad – Dr. Willie Morrow

TABLE of CONTENTS

- Preface

- Introduction

- Strength and the Expectations of Being Strong - Embrace the Season

- Tender, Soft, Self-Care, and Reflection - Be Good To You

- Cognitive Connectivity - No Boundaries to Heal

- Moving Forward - Sort Through The Pieces

- The Interest of Investigation - Setting the Appropriate Boundaries

- Giving Voice to the Inner Little Girl - Not Then but Now

- Your Strength, Your Truth - Ready or Not It's Me

- Woman. Wounded. Warrior. - You Can't Fit My Shoes

- The Transformation and The Healing - Dive Into Emotional Intelligence

KUJICHAGULIA
Greetings!

Samella England was born in San Leandro CA and has been in San Diego since the age of 3. A few of her over comings consist of racism, molestation, a drug addicted parent, her own alcoholism, teenage pregnancy, struggling with her own confidence, divorces, homelessness, and after all that rising again to help others.

Samella is a mother. She has mentored many young mothers and teens for 2 decades. She identifies with these women through their situations, conditions, looks, and experiences. She speaks to their hearts and empowers these ladies with the transforming approach through "Emotional Intellect."

Samella runs her own organization and Community platform in order to Inspire and see change in the lives of mothers and youth. She maintains and stays focus on reaching, strengthening and empowering those that are traveling the path that she has walked. Samella believes that what she has learned over the years will help single moms and young ladies of all ages. Helping the youth and women to understand that our battles are not on a combat, hand to hand level. It's often challenging yet worthwhile.

Enhancing their intellectual level with knowledge while focusing on their leadership abilities will help shape their futures. Driving their appreciation and discipline in their thoughts and actions instilling Dedication, Reliability and Integrity to carry them a long way as they're raising their children. As a business owner with treatment counselor and case manager skills while assisting families that experience chronic homelessness and again give back where she sees the need through educating, encouraging and empowering. For over 20 years she's worked with other mompreneurs to be an example to those that must learn how to own their motherhood status, especially when they are single. Samella continues to reach out to schools and organizations that have mothers that are feeling "some kind of way" due to the fact that they truly have no one that they identify with as I stand in as the identity of past hurt and present success, inspiring them to be more while being that ear that they can talk to and face of encouragement. The overall purpose of this e-book is to show our similarities and prove our resilience.

Best regards,

Courageous Changer
Samella England

PREFACE

Every move that an individual makes eventually comes with consequences or rewards. Being a black woman raised in white society has not been easy. When I begin to see the world in a different light, is sometime in elementary school. I noticed the only influential black shows on television at that time was the Cosby Show and then in time birthed A Different World. Prior to these two shows I remember watching the television show Fame which featured the black dance instructor Debbie Allen and at least one maybe two other black actors. Though these were positive black images there was something missing, something I needed to know more about.

To not truly know you, your heritage, your culture, your tribe, your language, your traditions is a life pursuing journey. And then the ancestors call and surround you with their presence, love, light, and spiritual wisdom. Let me assure you that some things are just DNA'd into the blood stream. Without hesitation I seek my roots.

PREFACE

My roots are what keeps me planted and empowers me to remain with what I know and the leading of my ancestors. When I engage with the white washed black it is evident how I need to move around that individual. How can an original black woman be original without being true to herself? How can she be true to herself without knowing herself? Breaking out of our mental boxes and entrapments, learning our behaviors, setting healthy boundaries, knowing our strength, truths, being good to you, and giving voice to the inner little girl that we all have no matter our age, is an important element of remaining true to our roots.

My book, **The Art of Remaining: Practical Foundations for the Culture and Heritage of the Colored Women** is a manual to simply help change your experience while going through your seasons. And when you run across a page to implement your thoughts take that time to defragment your thoughts and get to the core of you, transparently.

INTRODUCTION

This book will be read by millions because everyone truly would love to understand how the black woman is able to stand the test of every season even when she is not emotionally or mentally connected with situations that we have faced. Not only in our live as a black woman yet the lives of those who were, are, and to come. We also stand "strong" through the lives of our friends, mentees, and families. Does the black woman ever have the opportunity of just being, being human? Often times the societal system has caused the black woman to raise the children by herself. Or deal with the perversion of dysfunctional men and the expectations that we put upon men, have too many times caused us to overly express or numb ourselves to the feelings of sadness, madness, anger, frustrations, depression, heartbreak or simply the feeling of "I don't know" and we will often admit that we don't care, yet we do.

XII

Many of us as the black woman have high expectations of our men. Though we should and very reasonable, yet they have been trapped. Now ladies I need you to hear me. It is not that they, the men, cannot fulfill request. The truth of the matter is that yes, they have long lasting stamina yet, men are not multi taskers like us. In this American society we have been taught to look at our men as if they are the ones with the ability to perform more than one task efficiently at a time. When we are the dominates in coming home taking care of the children, cooking dinner, and still have enough to lullaby him to sleep. Ladies' men are more focused driven, you know straight to the "heart" of whatever matter. Where we can framework any situation of all circumstances. We can make sense out of what truly happened when all sort of pieces are missing from the puzzle. I know y'all know what I'm talking about! So why does the black woman frustrate herself? We have forgotten our foundation! Better yet we don't know. "We don't know our story." No true knowledge of our culture? And far too often we lack the self-esteem and pride of being an indigenous / black woman, a Queen of many nations.

We were stolen and are left with figuring out who we are. Who are you as a woman? You are the neck that causes that man's head to spin. You are the pillow and voice of reason that can soothe all of his doubts and fears. You are neither a stepping stool nor an old welcome mat. Ladies you have an important and powerful role and once you truly realize who you are no one can take you out of the order of life.

The Art of Remaining is to encourage those who have been looking for simple answers. This is for the woman who is truly over fighting the miscommunication battle in and outside of self. This is for the woman who is truly looking for and need to understand her purpose. For the woman who is not ready to give up and need to reconnect to her roots and culture via transparency! Ladies there is an old saying that goes, "It's not what you say but how you say it." Ladies sometimes we are so naughty when communicating with our men and others because of our Reflectatory Love, frustration with "the" situation, and tired of being tired of what's next and with not knowing self-identity.

XIV

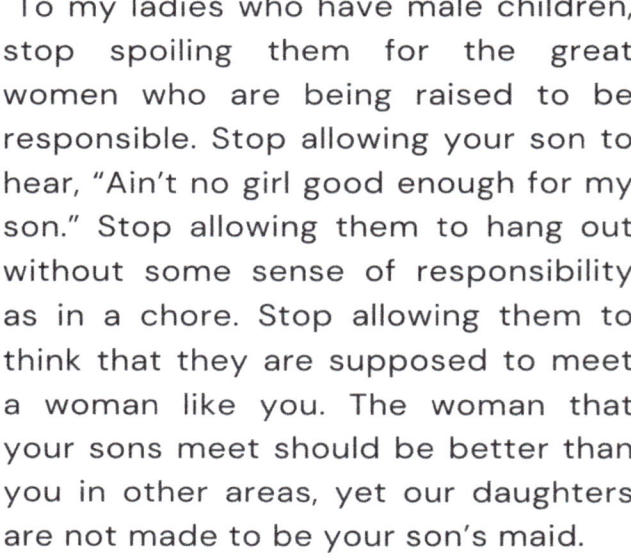

To my ladies who have male children, stop spoiling them for the great women who are being raised to be responsible. Stop allowing your son to hear, "Ain't no girl good enough for my son." Stop allowing them to hang out without some sense of responsibility as in a chore. Stop allowing them to think that they are supposed to meet a woman like you. The woman that your sons meet should be better than you in other areas, yet our daughters are not made to be your son's maid.

Tupac said it best that," we would have a race of babies who would disrespect the ladies!" Please my dear sisters teach your sons how to cook, clean, and treat a woman. And remind him that if he isn't ready to be a father, jimmy hat that thang just like I tell my girls. Also, please help him to embrace the great difference between his mommy and his woman

Yes, ladies we have so many conversations to have yet first it starts with how we treat ourselves, how we love ourselves, and how we take care of ourselves!

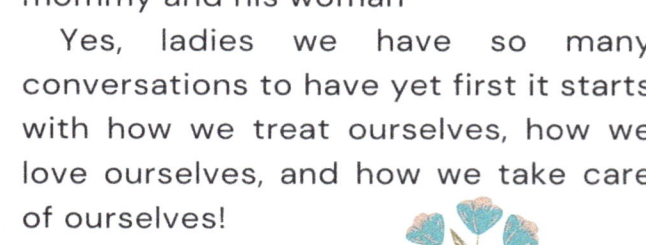

Read It Twice

Many of us as the black woman have high expectations of our men. Though we should and very reasonable, yet they have been trapped. Now ladies I need you to hear me. It is not that they, the men, cannot fulfill request. The truth of the matter is that yes, they have long lasting stamina yet, men are not multi taskers like us. In this American society we have been taught to look at our men as if they are the ones with the ability to perform more than one task efficiently at a time. When we are the dominates in coming home taking care of the children, cooking dinner, and still have enough to lullaby him to sleep. Ladies' men are more focused driven, you know straight to the "heart" of whatever matter. Where we can framework any situation of all circumstances. We can make sense out of what truly happened when all sort of pieces are missing from the puzzle. I know y'all know what I'm talking about! So why does the black woman frustrate herself? We have forgotten our foundation! Better yet we don't know. "We don't know our story." No true knowledge of our culture? And far too often we lack the self-esteem and pride of being an indigenous / black woman, a **_Queen of many nations._**

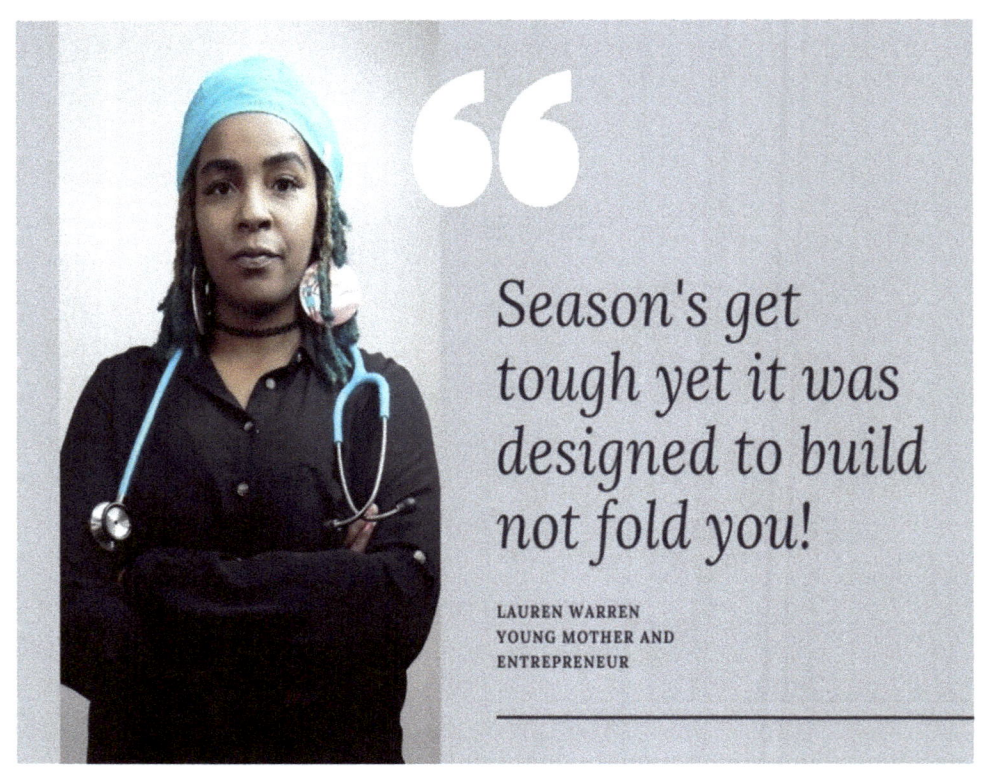

Write Words of Affirmation

XVII

STENGTH AND THE EXPECTATIONS OF BEING STRONG

EMBRACE THE SEASONS

Something's are unexpected while others are planned

Embrace The Seasons
1.

Far too many times we as women have been devalued or blatantly overlooked for showing our emotions or being emotional especially for those of us that they, the individuals in our lives, consider "strong." Why does that happen? You could be the one that the family looks to for advice because you appear to always hold it together. The family has never seen you cry, or you could be the crybaby yet there is an undeniable strength about you. You, the one that was teased, the "black sheep," the one who is often talked about, tolerated hardly celebrated, and criticized for everything you did and didn't do. You're the one that when things are right no one reaches out, yet the minute situations are haywire you are on recall, speed dial, mountain and standard time, the one who all of the sudden has all of the answers and you are the solution no matter how you would go about getting the outcome. "They," the accusers, just need for you to show up and be the irresponsible, massive, negative ball of energy, who "they" continually proclaim that you are.

Embrace The Seasons

Well, there are a few lessons that I have learned during life. One of the lessons is that as a person matures. Listen, I said mature not get older in age, as a person matures the brain development begins to accept, balance, embrace and pushes out the life experiences that we had no control over or the experiences that we have learned or are learning how to deal with, if we allow the change to evolve. An unbalanced or underdeveloped brain is stagnant and doesn't function at full capacity. Our life traumas, our childhood perspectives, our true fears and strengths are what threaded us. Many of us were brought up in the sweep it under the carpet households. You know the era of, what goes on in this house stays in this house! We have now embarked upon a generation of 40 something year olds who have become open with their children. Many of these 40-year-olds work on keeping a foundation that somehow aided in keeping their minds yet underhandedly drove them crazy with all of the craziness that they seen growing up.

Embrace The Seasons

    We who are in our 40 and beyond didn't have time to sit in the corner and complain about what we did and didn't have. We didn't have time to bawl up in the corner and cry about our current situations and many other circumstances that we had absolutely no control over. We learned how to press through because though we didn't realize it at that time, yet it has always been sink or swim just like the many generations before us. Yet, today's gen is folding under pressures of such things like not having weed to smoke. Now if this isn't the most cunning trick of the deceivers I don't know what is.

    Now you placed someone that has been through watching a mom being beat by her boyfriend. Or maybe a child who watched the cheating ways of the father and the depression that set in on the household because the mom was submerging in her own false images of what the strength of the woman truly looked like. Or someone who had to watch her siblings leave the house due to the domestic violence that her siblings couldn't protect the mother from. Or someone who actually fought toe to toe not shot the people of the same color and culture in the neighborhood no matter how many blocks away it was fist to fist.

Embrace The Seasons

There was a generation of people who believed that only the cowards carried the guns and shot for the easy win. A generation of individuals who had to learn what the hell it meant to have an orgasm somewhere in their mid 30's because they had been molested for years by individuals in their houses and family dynamics. And those of us who have been able to achieve the point of forgiving the predators, ignorant family members, unlearnt mothers and fathers and yet balance out our purpose. And then attempt to stand us against the individuals who cry because they don't have blunt paper or weed to smoke or everyone who uses their diagnoses as excuses for not accomplishing the purpose of their existence.

Yes, we, the generation that I was brought up in and the generations before me, were taught how to be strong without words. We were taught through the action of the adults who protected and the ones who were supposed to protect and assure that we were safe. The true issue is that this hamster wheel is still running, and the deceivers have made the younger generation believe that the solution is in the herbs and the herbs alone. Though there is healing in the herbs yet if you are not balanced and have not had an opportunity to self-reflect on your bullshit, traumas, cares and concerns than the herbs will never truly bring peace as the culture intended.

Embrace The Seasons

    Trust me, when you see a black woman in tears it is not because she is weak. There isn't a weak muscle or bone in our bodies! If I went into the intricate functionality of being a woman, some would rethink on attempting to ever bring the disrespectful energy to any born, monthly menstrual, tender breasted, birth bearing, and mother of life. When we are in tears it is often for nations who no longer know who they are. A nation who has forgotten the women place as the prophet Tupac Shukar stated years ago "Ladies keep your head up!" Tupac also stated, "that if you as the men don't begin to heal the women, be real to the women, that there will be a race of babies that will hate the ladies, that makes the babies." We as women have every right to take a break, to say NO, to make everyone around us grow up, to always set the boundaries, and to never feel guilty about being the navigator of the nations. We have every right to transfer from mommy to mother, to never be the mother to some grow man who has mommy issues, to teach as the nurturer and the task master. We have raised children from the white slave house to the dark in house and yet individuals dare to undermine the elegant strength of first the black women and then women in general. Bringing it to today's lingual, shaken my head, periodt.

    I learned how to embrace the season's that I was chosen to go through and endure. Nothing has been perfect, yet the lessons are irreplaceable and have caused me to stand courageous against all odds.

Unapologetic Feminine Energy

XXIII

TENDER, SOFT, SELF- CARE, AND REFLECTION

BE GOOD TO YOU

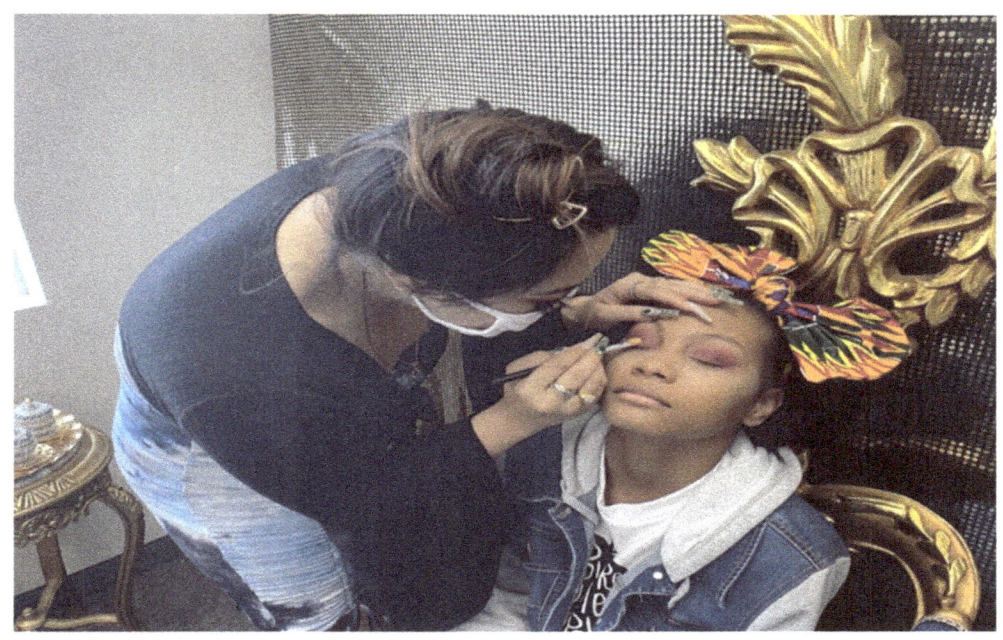

Something's are unexpected while others are planned

Be Good To You
2.

 The softness of a pillow or smooth feeling of (55 % cotton, 43% polyester and 2% spandex) felt clothing and the squishiness of a tension ball or the comfort of the warmth of a lovable fluffy blanket are things that we can experience without any feedback except for our own. If you have ever been acquainted with your sense of feelings than you can identify with how awesome these things feel to your touch receptor.

 There are times in life that we have to allow ourselves to feel as good if not better than the fabrics and things described above. With this being said you must know that you should not allow anyone to treat you worse than you treat yourself.

 Now you know what the problem is right? Come on ladies I'll give you all at least one guess. The problem is that most of us as women don't know how to treat ourselves. I know that some are in disagreement yet it's the truth. Okay, so let me asked you a few questions. Start a timer and be honest with how long it takes you to answer these questions about yourself.

Be Good To You

know you | or not

1) What is your favorite color?

2) Pick one food that's your favorite?

3) If you were asked to pick a restaurant to eat at, where would you go?

4) Would you get depressed because your man didn't buy you flowers? If yes, why?

5) Do you truly know what makes you happy? What?

6) Do you like or love you?

Be Good To You

Okay, honestly, how long did it take you to answer those 5 questions about, you? ___hr _____mins.

Did you take hours or minutes to answer the questions? Some women get stuck on just thinking about their favorite color. These basic questions are important because it will help you in finding a balance with yourself. After all this entire book is for us ladies. Once we regain a balance on who we truly are and not what the society has plagued us, we will align up which in turn will cause everyone around us to get in line. We must take back who and what we are as the mother of life and givers of birth. Women we give and give and give some more which means that no one has the right to disrespect the ordained vessels and purpose that we must fulfill.

Be Good To You

So, what does "being good" to you look like? Well, let's take a minute to think. Okay, we all have our ideas as to what being good looks like yet the experience of it to many is unfamiliar. List at least five things that you do to be good to you. Go ahead, I'll wait.

a.

b.

c.

d.

e.

Alright, so just take a minute to self-reflect. Even get a mirror if you need to because it's time to have a conversation with yourself. Are you ready? Now ask yourself when was the last time you've completed at least one of the thoughts that you wrote. Listen ladies, balance is everything. This is why individuals study the Chakra Healing Chart while others may find their balance through Tai Chi. Both of these are a form of art which require skill. Two of the main skills are focus and the willingness to change certain things to gain the ultimate end of balance to perform the art rather the fight is physical or mental. Both arts bring a balance when applied correctly.

Be Good To You

Ladies this is why we must have a balance within ourselves? How many times have we been left with holding not only our bags yet the children luggage's as well while the man is off into the wind? Hear me when I say that there are times when we must allow a man to be a man by not nagging him or making him feel as bad as the society have already made him feel. We as black women have seen through the eyes of the ancestors and history our men raped, beaten, belittled, tortured, and now up to speed brought to the forefront where they now refer to us as "bitches." A degrading title given to women and black women from the plantation yet widely acceptable by the society.

Be Good To You

Ladies by the show of hands how many of us are asking to be feed, petted, and housed without putting forth our best efforts to assure that we are supporting and standing by the black man as we have done for age in and out? Black man the black woman, the original indigenous black woman has always had your back. Especially when massa, the society, has whipped it. For too long we have allowed the hand that has feed you to be bitten and now we go back to the foundation, the roots, which many of us, as original women, have never left, heart and soul.

Be Good To You

These are some of the reasons why we must take care of and be good to ourselves ladies! We are always on the battlefield as the care giver and when the care giver is down who is there to retrieve her? Back in the days the women have always been there for each other. Not in a sexual obstinate, let me show you how to love you better than a man, but on sisterly sister I love you. I understand what you're going through and I am here as a listening ear and sounding board because 'you are my sister.'

Unapologetic Foundation

XXXI

COGNITIVE CONNECTIVITY

NO BOUNDARIES TO HEAL

Something's are unexpected while others are planned

No Boundaries to Heal
3.

I was raised in the C.O.G.I.C. denomination. I know about speaking in unknown tongues, jumping on the back of demons to cast out all ungodly spirits, to dancing and running around the church. Most of the time no one is chasing you unless someone decided to wear some sleazy high split loose bra dress to impress the pastor or somebody else's man. When this happens the ushers or maybe the church mother's having to chase the woman with a sheet to help the men stay "saved." My God! This is most of the unmentioned side yet there is a side of holiness that many must learn and apply. I remember before I would leave my house, I would do a praise check in the mirror. Oh, what is a praise check? Well because I am a dancer I would stand in front of a mirror to clap my hands and bounce around a little bit. Being a curvaceous woman, I know how and what will get a man or men attention. I have a commonsense respect for not only the church where we joined to fellowship and my physical body "church," yet the respect that of love that the bible talks about "Agape." Agape for me means, sister and brother I love you so much that I am going to do my best not to offend you. When I do my best, holy spirit lead, yet someone is still offended I learned that it's not my issue it is actually a personal problem within that person.

No Boundaries to Heal

Though the Church of God In Christ was not the first religion I was introduced to I enjoyed being part of that culture. It was never a dull moment when I attended. From the God given talent of the praise team and choirs to the manifested word that came from the pulpit. There was a time when my world only truly existed around living completely for the one track of the C.O.G.I.C culture. My complete submission to this season helped me get through my sister getting killed in the car accident, me having to fight for my nieces and nephew, and having to be balanced as a young mother without true personal mother guidance, and yet being able to truly acknowledge God as my maker, father, peace giver, comforter and sustainer. This is just a few things that God has been to me.

No Boundaries to Heal

When I first started learning about religion my mother was actually practicing a chanting religion "nam-myoho-renge-kyo." I still have no idea what that meant yet my mother appeared to be at peace. At this time, we lived in Point Loma. I was in elementary school and at some point, I was beaten by some of the white kids that attended Loma Portal Elementary. Low and behold their family were part of the white cowards that wore cloth on their heads and because I was just about the only black child at the school, they decided to form a circle around me, kick, spit, and devalue me by calling me a little nigger which at that time I had no idea what that word meant. They told me to go back where I belonged. Well, at that time in the 2nd or 3rd grade if I knew my history, I probably would have reminded them that their selfish ancestors are the ones who brought my ancestors here to till, work, and build the very land that they were beating me on.

 ## No Boundaries to Heal

    When I was able to get away from the many abuses that I experienced in the home that I was raised I ended up pregnant at 15 and living with my big sister. Prior to me being pregnant and hanging out with my big sis I ended up attending the Mosque with her and learning some of the ways of the American Islam through the eyes of the Honorable Louis Farrakhan. Okay, so let me drop this for us really quick. Rather we as the black culture know or believe this or not the society, white slave government, believes that the Honorable Louis Farrakhan is the entire American black cultures leader. Uh, oh, please don't smack your lips or roll your eyes at the messenger, me. The main example is who else was able to pull a million plus men and women together during a weekday to make a stand for the Million-Man March? So now with facts we can now agree to disagree, yet Farrakhan drops truth on top of truth, and I absolutely respect him and the vessel that he embodies.

    Now back to the true basis of this chapter. In spite of my many roads that I have had to travel by choice or by force I have come to the realization that it is all by design. The design is never there to destroy; it is always there to build. If we again, are not balanced enough to recognize that, "this is just a season," whatever your, "this season," is ladies you will end up in the tailspin of the mental break down and the uncomfortability of being inside of your own skin. With many of today's men we must always wear our suit and tie. Keep the shirt buttoned all the way to the top. Wear the pants fitted yet loose or the skirt to the top of the knees so that we are not so inviting into our sexiness as we are holding meaningful conversations.

No Boundaries to Heal

There are many ways to place boundaries in order to walk as "the women" of the foundation which we are made from. Yet we have to get our minds and emotions controlled. Ladies, there are times when we must disconnect from our emotions to implement the game plan. It's always okay to cry, if that is what gets you through and keep you from choking people out. However, while the tears drop and while you're feeling every alternative emotion, think about the next steps to moving forward and to your next level. Open your mind to heal. I have learned so much from being exposed to different religions, people, and the exposures of true cultures. I made a decision years ago that I would not allow anyone to bind me to religion. I will consciously keep my relationship with the God in and outside of me to continue to be the willing and purposeful vessel I have been designed as.

No Boundaries to Heal

With knowing your own story, exposures, and experiences write you a promise in order to keep you from the fears of being free within your own skin. Write a promise that will enable you to rise to your complete and full potential. A promise to shape you into the lover of first yourself and then to the individuals that you must show what love truly is. Use the next page to reflect on what process you will begin to use to cause your brain and emotions to function at a higher-level. As you continue to read this book you will gain more knowledge and comprehension of who you are as a woman. We don't have a weak bone or muscle in our bodies so we must use them to full capacity while we possess the ability to assure that as we grow up, everyone that surrounds us must also grow up with the skills to problem-solve, learn the critical importance of response and not reacting, and as much common sense and common courtesy as feasible.

Audaciously Healing

XXXVIII

No Boundaries to Heal

Reflection Writing:

With a trustworthy, non-judgmental, transparent, sensitive yet firm bestie

(List 3 to 5 things that you can work on to bring forth your healing and laughter)

XXXIX

MOVING FORWARD

SORT THROUGH THE PIECES

Something's are unexpected while others are planned

Sort Through The Pieces
4.

 We all have puzzle pieces to our stories. As children we saw things that happened. Or we seen things that we thought happened. Because the mind can only see things from an age perspective, as children we seen situations and felt concerns yet our obscured views. Due to us not being able to knowledgably verbalize what we felt our feelers were in full affect which is why that person that was doing harm to us came around we already knew that they were there to harm us. Babies are usually real good at showing us that some type of predator is in our presence. No mind you a predator isn't always of a sexual nature. Predators are those who 'prey on others' on so many levels.

 One of the reasons why we have difficulties moving forward is because we are always trying to put together the obscured puzzle. Now there are some who have incomprehensible memories. I have run into people that stated that they can remember situations from when they were babies frame by frame. I haven't ran into many people who has an extensive memory from childhood as babies yet since geniuses exist I give the benefit of assurance to those who proclaim to have such a vast memory. However, the majority of us see dimly through the glass of our memories. When we get to our teen years we begin to mix up stories and cause those stories to become our reality.

Sort Through The Pieces

Listen, those things that we must sort through are so evident in the way that we treat ourselves and the way that we treat others. The way that we can get off of the hamster wheel of our own ridiculous cycle is by standing toe to toe with the realities that we can change, bring truth to, let go, or make better for the next generation. Often times we live rooted in the past instead of plucking the weeds. I have come to the conclusion that many haven't figured out, that sometimes they just desire to be mad. Why do you think that they start arguments, why do you think that they play the victim, why do you think that they want to put their insecurities on you, why do you think that they deflect every situation opposed to looking at the part that they played in the narrative? Now, yes all of us have so mental situations to deal with. Yet, "the society," desire for all of us to fall into the hands of the deceiver and become stagnant, which is why "the society" need for all of us to buy into their awkward way of thinking.

Sort Through The Pieces

The ancestors left us with the common sense that we, as black women, used to raise the children of the society, the massa's children. Though battered, misused, rejected, defiled, underestimated, and often referred to as the ignorant we were able to handle what the society, massa, never could, their own households.

Sort Through The Pieces

Now their non-sense has run over into the streets and the relentlessness of the ones looking for direction have gravitated and gripped their set-up and destructive plot. So, we as indigenous women have inadvertently rejected our children and pushed them into the streets as we were caused to first do to our men and vice versa with simple entanglements of the minds of our men with simple tantalizing commercials such as Burger King, "have it your way." Somebody please help me understand what a naked woman has to do with a burger? Here it is again massa's mentality of looking at women firstly like a piece of meat. Secondly, sinking the "perfectly" imperfect shaped Caucasian women as the vision of how all women should look. This thirdly, creates the trap impressed upon the black man mindset, that white women are better than black women. I know that you cannot see the bigger conspiracy, yet this is how many of the ideas are formed, subtle hypnosis. This has become one of the many avenues for the entrapment for the man mentality. Subtle things like this that men have become desensitized to because it has become the norm. Over sexualization aids in his unawareness of continuous disrespect of the black women. Now what has been created is not only the disrespect by sight yet by verbalization.

Sort Through The Pieces

I have zoned in on the fact that not everyone understands that many women have accepted the devaluation of not just being looked at and appreciated as pieces of meat yet being called a female dog, the bitch. Oh, not just the bitch, it's Ms. or Mrs. Bitch! Note to yourself, not all women like to be looked at like pieces of fined cooked sirloin and not all women are going to engage with you on the "bitch" level. Often times the word is used due to us putting our foot down, setting boundaries. Another nickname given by massa yet accepted by the masses. Now remember we are just sorting through some of the pieces. The pieces that are actually unfavorable on many mental and emotional levels, nevertheless, "bitch," is yet mentally captured as a righteous and attractive word. Look I have a great aunt who primarily reminds me of how proud she is of me. She also reminds me that I am a leader and not a follower. Third, that if a person is not feeding, fucking, nor supporting me than don't concern myself with their opinions. This I pass on to you. This I share with you because I am one of many who are in the class of, "No, sirs or ma'ams you cannot impose upon me your label, and you can look at me like sirloin if you desire yet our business will stay above the waist. And men be sure to look at me in my eyes when you're talking with me, or I will become your reflection." Where are the ladies who are taking this stance?

Sort Through The Pieces

The bottom line is that one may not understand why they function in certain ways yet being aware of foundations and where things started and how our ancestors made it over with not falling into the trap was and will always be important. A man learning what is in my brain before diving into a full fledge body wave of getting to know my clitoris is very important and a topic that is over the heads of many women and most men. Individuals truly are not ready to acknowledge the part that we as women play in falling for the trap that brings to life that part of a woman which aids in countless decision making, this round.

Sort Through The Pieces

Yeah, I didn't learn these important self-reflectatory skills until I experienced the situations, circumstances, and honestly got to know me. Not knowing me just from a societal and circle point of view which helped me to understand my Jah given purpose, years later. This skilled kicked in at my 20's when my mom expressed to me for the last time that she would no longer apologies for the things that she did and didn't do. You know the short comings that we as folks love to hold people in contempt to? Note to yourself, we become "we" through the stories of our transformations, remaining true to "us," and not following the status quo. One of my favorites and many observations is that we, as people, start off in life only expressing the love that we were shown to express. If I was shown abuse of any sort then my love will be abusive, rather subtle or overly recognizable, the love is shown. Understanding that seasons were there to grow and growing past any season that harmed is one of the most imperative investigations of self and surrounding that I have ever accomplished through my God given, not manmade, relationships. This is what made my relationship with my internal God and external God so unique. Everyone isn't going to get why you do what you do yet you have better understand why you do and don't do what you and do don't. The old mothers of the church would say " baaybay, stand for something or fall for anything." My findings through exploring the science of sorting through the pieces is to always acknowledge God and keep "man" in the "how is she and what is she doing," stage of moving forward.

Stealth Identity

XLVII

THE INTEREST OF INVESTIGATION

SETTING THE APPROPRIATE BOUNDARIES

Something's are unexpected while others are planned

Setting the Appropriate Boundaries
5.

Setting boundaries are very important in our lives. Setting Healthy Boundaries is another level of consciousness that few exercise. There are distinctions between boundaries and healthy boundaries. What are the distinctions? Within in boundaries there are elements of favoritism. Within healthy boundaries there are "across the board of our life" decisions that one has to come to terms with which will assist that person to remain balanced. I do not have an issue with having a substantive relationship with myself. I also am aware that if my mind is not in a state of peace within and after a decision then I will be in a battle with myself.

One of my interesting greatest accomplishments was having the opportunity of raising four girls to whom I refer to as my Queens. Now they come in sets and they were born in two different eras of my life. My first set was born during my TJ clubbing, transferring off of welfare, running my own daycare, discovering me, studying people and their motives, chasing peace, consistent rocky relationships from my mom and men, death of a sibling, I don't care attitude, going to different schools, fighting for my nephew and nieces, healing from sexual traumas, and the list goes on. My second set was born during my I had enough of this shit, casual social gathers, in and out of multi-level opportunities, fighting more mentally then physically, seeing people motives and intents, exercising my fair firm consistent habits and decisions, working consistently while building businesses, explaining situations to my first set, desiring a better relationship with my mom and very dominant mentality towards men, and in the midst of all that I didn't reveal I had been married three times including twice to the same man attempting to make a stable relationship work for our daughters. Notice ladies I didn't selfishly or out of anger say my or his girls, I wrote "our" daughters in spite of…

Setting the Appropriate Boundaries

I did not list bits of my life for show and tell. I listed it so that we women can understand that we all have a story and yet it is our responsibility to work our shit out as healthy as possible. Some may go and sit in the chair of a great aunt, while other may go and lay on the couch of a stranger. Some may join a group that have accepted and loved on them, while others may write in a journal. Your method is just that yours while remembering that we as black women come from a rooted lineage of strength, dignity, creativity, courage, stubbornness, humble, painful, and unrelentless pride. It took a humbleness, strength, creativity, courage and pride to lead the Underground Railroad. Here are a few more names that we may or may not have heard of yet gave into their purpose to be a victor not into the pain of a victim, Del. Eleanor Norton, Nina Simone, Mae Jemison, Misty Copeland, Madam C.J. Walker, Rosa Parks, Dorothy Height, Diane Nash, Debbie Allen, Michelle Obama, and many, many more who stood on the blood of our ancestors strength and knowledge and made the decision to press on without the systemic couch method of recovery. They made their decisions and allowed the pains and traumas to strengthen not weaken. I'm sure that they understood the state of "about to lose my mind." I'm sure that these women understood sacrifice and leaving people yet re-rounding to see if they were ready to move. I am certain that each one of these women understood that Art of Remaining, free, victor, transparent, in love for the sake of love, focused, relentless, humble pride, and moving in silence.

<u>Setting the Appropriate Boundaries</u>

The point of the history and recollection list is that we have to get the bad stuff out in order for any good seeds to enter, plant, die and grow. Setting healthy boundaries can be a difficult part of our lives yet it can assist with some of the embarrassing negative talks that a woman conjures from being inside of her head for too long. Self-poor image and reflection of what society and experience of life has feed her, men have given her, and those thoughts and vibrations she continuously feed off of.

Now, how do we as women change our paradigm? Of course, we all have our idealistic reality of what restructure and shifting of the mindset looks like yet there is a written formula that one can use and implement as one moves forward to healing and setting healthy boundaries by giving voice to the inner little girl through The Potted Plant Method!

Sincerely Outside the Box

GIVING VOICE TO THE INNER LITTLE GIRL

NOT THEN BUT NOW

Something's are unexpected while others are planned

Not Then But Now

6.

As I thought about this chapter, I could feel my throat thickening and tears attempting to fill my eyes. Let me take you back to me and my oldest sis who was my ride and die, we took a picture before going out to perform at a club that she frequented. That sister right there, was the Cookie that didn't crumble for anything or anyone. We could be pissed off at each other yet let there be some static, all it took was one call and we were there for each other. My sister was very instrumental in many of my life situations from a baby on up. She was at most part my protection and then at other parts, crazy to say my opponent. I think that she was so used to protecting me that whenever I showed my independence, rather ideas or movements, it would overwhelm her or was some type of trigger. You may know someone similar in your life, please note that you're not the direct trigger and if you have a hard time setting boundaries then you should seek help.

Not Then But Now

    I learnt and seen the effects of being dependent after a certain age and how that dependency is very unhealthy. You can link this comment back to making everyone else around us grow up back in chapter 1. As a little girl I looked up to a few people and some of those same people that I was looking up to were the ones who hurt me and some of the hurt was worse than others. Most of y'all are aware of what I am talking about.

    *Now let me take a minute and say that if you are reluctant on moving forward to a true tool to use to assist in your healing you may desire to have someone with you if you're by yourself or you may desire to have a self-pep check talk to assure that you can move forward within yourself. If you believe that you need a counselor or a trusted friend to get through this process, please do so. Don't be afraid to cry, get upset, feel withdrawn, or naked. Don't be afraid to feel bold, courageous, relentless, or fearless. These are healing feeling, the true part of the healing that you are about to experience. This is the shedding or coming out of that mental box that some people will make you or attempt to make you feel guilty about. If I don't feel sad there is something wrong with me? When a person has come to a point in their life of truly understanding that there is nothing to fear but fears, then one understands that the unsaddened bold, relentless little girl who only knew how to work out of fear from not being protected has found protection, her worth, and her voice so she has no reason to fear anything as she heals. *

Not Then But Now

So, the hurt that we were about to get into starts where and with who? Did you notice that I didn't say "your" hurt? That is because this healing comes with a mindset change. The way that we perceive, the way that we think, the way that we give attention and energy to binding vibrations causes us to remain in binding situations. Listen I am no Mary Johnson yet once I begin to break out of barriers because firstly I kept and keep a dignified relationship with Jah, Allah, God and realized the warp speed magnitude that the bondage broke off of my life, mindset, and space I allowed no one to place me there again. The best that anyone can do in the healing space that I exercise is offer some proven suggestions from true "black" experience and allow me to consider what they are saying. Listen ladies when I show you what God gave me you will truly comprehend why I move the way that I move and why I make time for no drama and how I realize when one is still stuck in that unhealthy space and have yet to give her little girl a real voice.

__Not Then But Now__

Something as simple as a Potted Plant can speak depth to anyone who is listening and searching. The same way a butterfly has it's time of solidarity and come out as beautiful as a fresh smelling bunch of flowers is the same way you will come out once you realize and decide to use this tool. Allow the hurt little girl who desires to transform into a full productive free life giving spirit to take you on memory lane so that you can discover where many of your habits came from. Maybe it's being too honest, too emotional, too hard, too unfriendly, too manipulative, too naive, too nice, too you think you're better than, too it's my way or, too let me help you, too extraverted, too introverted, and the list can go on and on. Please remember that this healing is about you. This is not the time for you, the grown one, to begin to point fingers. This is time for you to have an open conversation with you because the little girl still lives on the inside. You just decided to tuck her away and act as if you don't cry at night when no one is looking. Or act as if you never just want to go back home because life at times have gotten real, real. Or sometimes wish that you can lay by your mom again and go back sometimes to your special place, wherever that was for you as a little girl.

Not Then But Now

It truly is okay that you didn't know how to deal with anything then, but now you are capable and I have the anointed wisdom to assist you. Now remember my earlier note, don't go any further if you're not ready.

Have you ever just looked at a Potted Plant? What is the first thing that you noticed?

Well, one of the many things that I noticed besides rather it is in a beautifully hand-crafted pottery or plastic are if the flowers are blooming. If the flowers have colors and what is the arrangement of the flowers. Are the flowers healthy and do they have a refreshing smell, no smell, or have they been sitting in stagnant water.

What is something's that you cannot see?

I observe that the foundation, roots, soil, nutrients, the last time it was watered, and how much life the plant has or doesn't have are invisible, along with some other microorganisms that assist the plant to grow. Because many of us are visual learners, I can show you what I am talking about better than I can tell you. Please note that even if you believe that you had the best childhood, balance is still needed if you suffer from emotional turbulences or mental discourse which we all do.

Not Then But Now

Diagram 1 – – Potted Plant Method

The Potted Plant Method

Not Then But Now

Diagram 2 - - Potted Plant Method

V
H
F

The Potted Plant Method

Not Then But Now

Diagram 3 - - Potted Plant Method

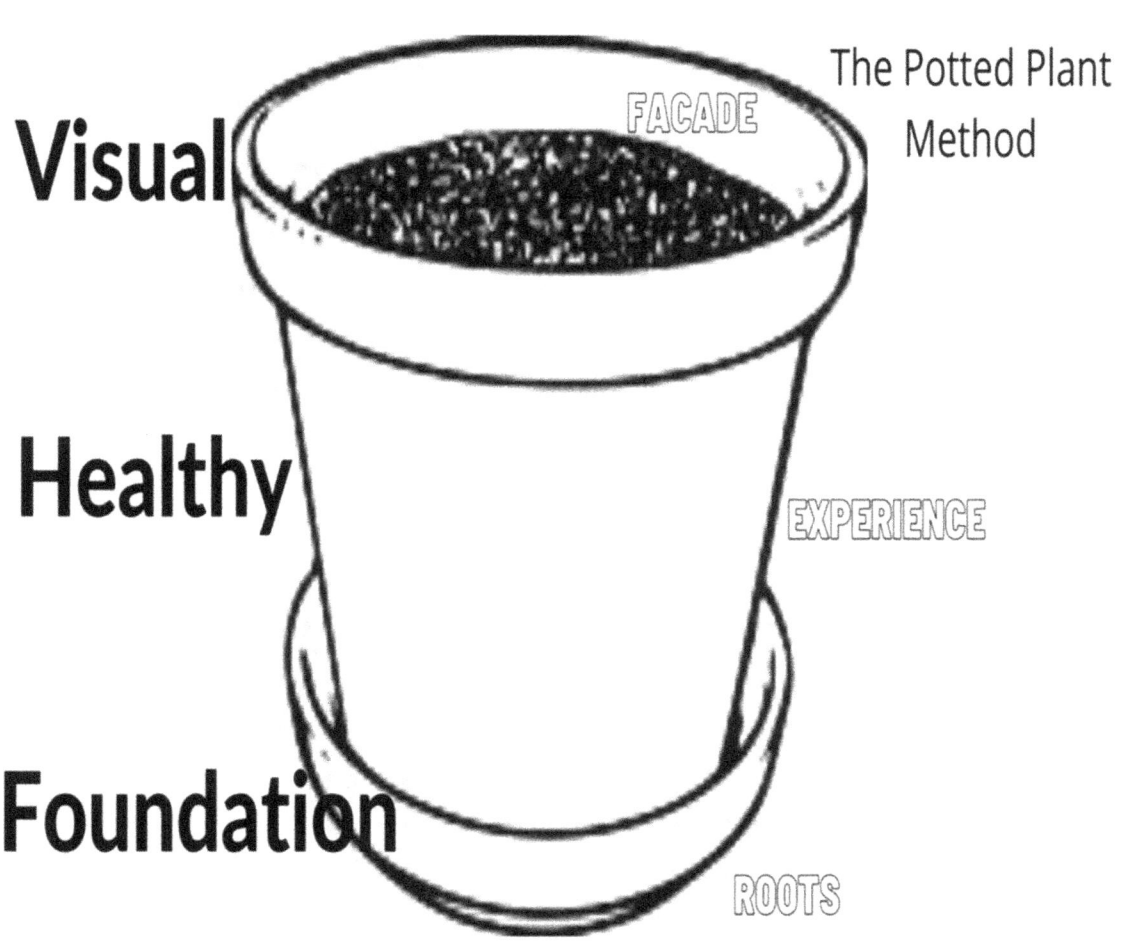

Not Then But Now

Diagram 4 – – Potted Plant Method

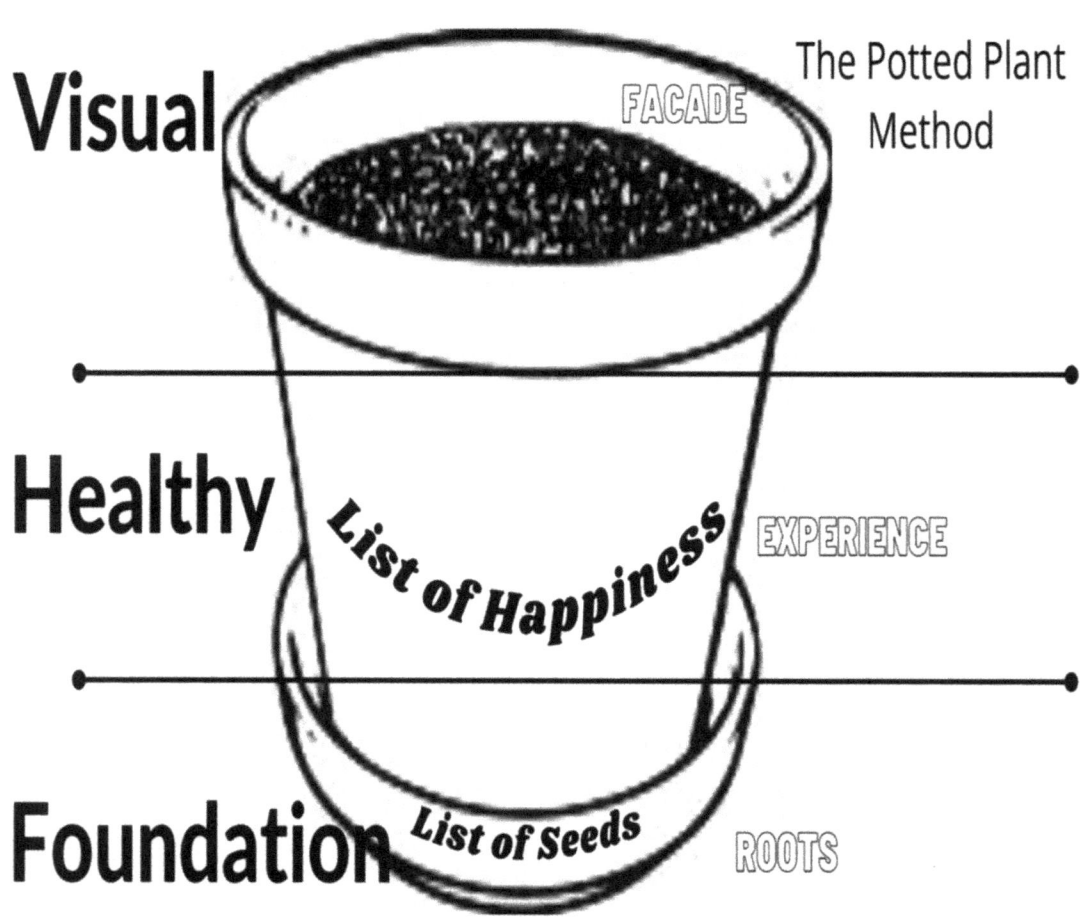

Not Then But Now

Diagram 5 - - Potted Plant Method

Not Then But Now

Diagram 6 - - Potted Plant Method

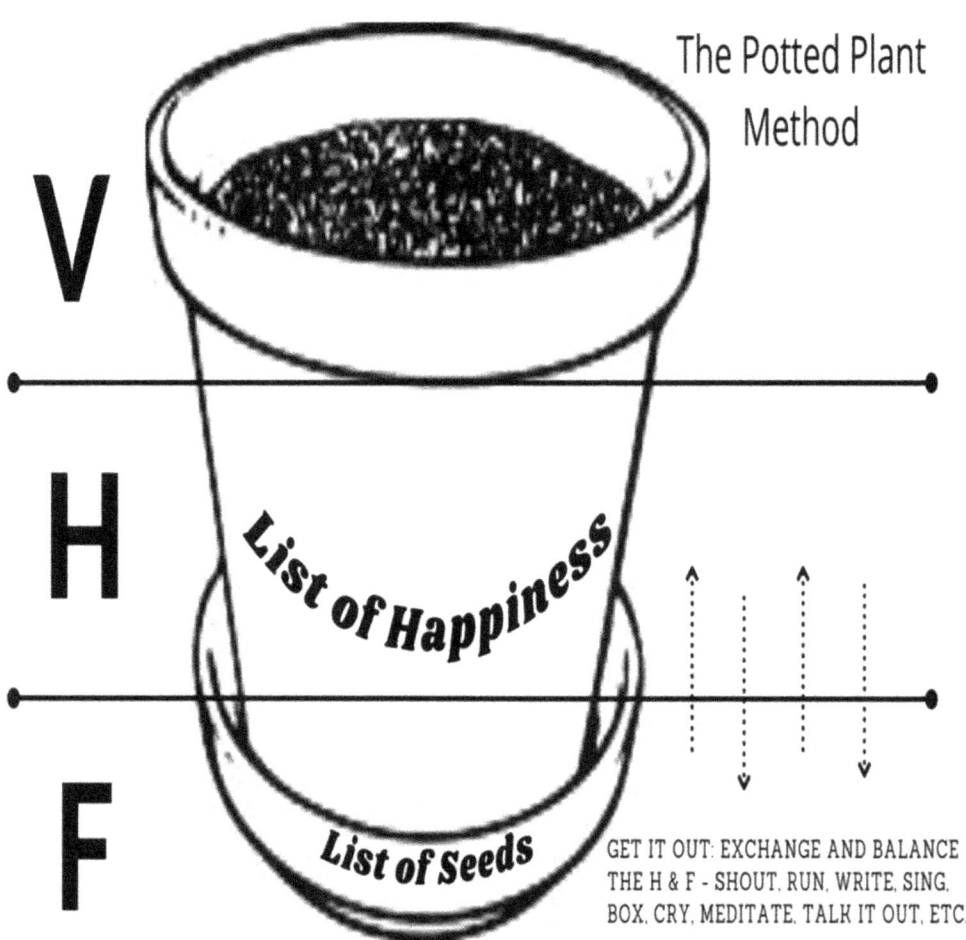

Not Then But Now

Diagram 7 - - Potted Plant Method

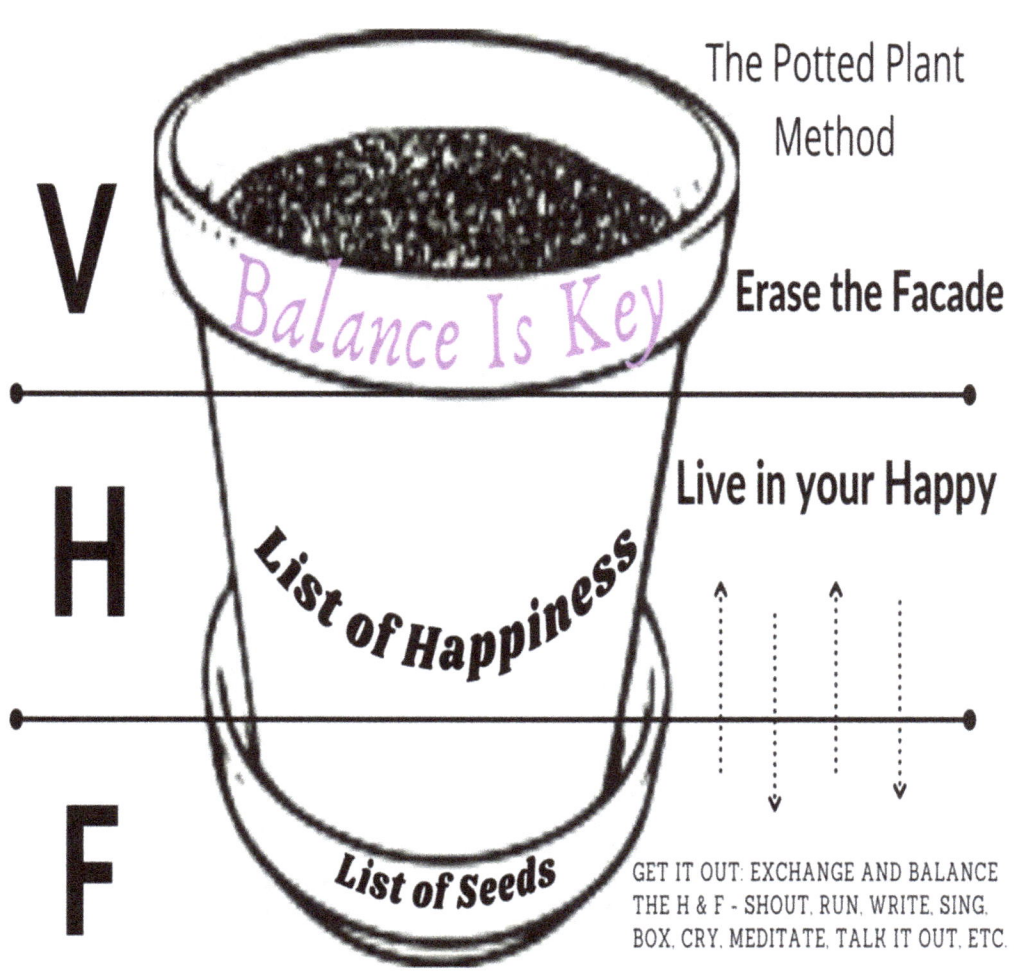

Not Then But Now

Balancing oneself is always the key to gaining a peace of mind. The Potted Plant is where Quaology Strategies begin to connect, and Emotional Intelligence is heightened. This is why Self-Reflectatory, meaning reflecting on you, oneself is very instrumental. You just charted out why you do and don't do the things that you do and don't do. Now how are you going to balance the things that you cannot change about your past with having the knowledge on how to balance and heal what you are bringing to your future? Communicate with self. Pray for self. Commit to self. Vibe and look towards God. Listen and talk to God. Allow the spirit, the ancestors, the great spiritual hymns, and roots of the confidence of trust in what you have learned from your story to guide you.. You have people waiting for you. Go where people are going to "Celebrate" you not where people are simply "Tolerating" you. Celebrate your failures, accomplishments, your life experiences, what you stand for, and what you are not willing to bow down to. Never allow anyone to dehumanize you. We all have imperfections. Don't let "them" fool you. Don't look for people to understand what they have not experienced or maybe had more support out of their condition then you did. People are not required to understand you, yet you're required to fulfill your purpose.

Continuous Equilibrium

LXV

YOUR STRENGTH, YOUR TRUTH

READY OR NOT IT'S ME

Something's are unexpected while others are planned

Ready Or Not It's Me

7.

When I step into a room, I immediately survey. I hone in on the energy, the vibrations, the leaders, the cliques, the ones who need the attention, the ones who are reserved, the confident and bold, and the volun-told and withdrawn. I walk into the room as the woman alpha that I have become. It could be because of mentors and brother taking me under their wings. Mentors and brothers like Dr. Willie Morrow, Tayari Howard, Ulysses "Simmie Braxton or Dr. Willie Blair who I meet much later in my entrepreneurial journey. These men never showed me intimidation moreover they never devalued me. There are many times that these men challenged me while encouraging the women that they saw me developing into.

Ready Or Not It's Me

One of my most memorable strength, truth, and mental transformations is when I was working at the Cannon Foundation. Years prior to this opportunity I'd already studied enough men to realize that many of them were so very disrespectful to women and I had enough. I remember walking into the auditorium of the Jacob's Center where Shane Harris was about to interview Nick. Mr. Cannon, Nick's father, needed to assure that everyone was on their post, so we had a quick meet up in front of the stage. When I walked into the room and as I stood in the circle of about seven, I felt their eyes on me. Their being the eyes of the men that was on me. I didn't make eye contact with each of the gentlemen who were staring at me yet I non-verbally communicated with at least five of them, eye to eye. Just as massa, the society, has taught many men that they can have any woman that they desire with some tired lines, manipulation, confidence, and pseudo security, I picked up and understand that making love to an individual's mind can grant access to many areas of one's life. The sexual tension of lust that many men exhibit, I begin to engage in the mindset and vibration. I realized that I could have him, him, him, him, and oh yeah him. Yet, my senses and mind frame at this time just needed to test the water that I knew that I had been treading.

Ready Or Not It's Me

Look though men and women are very different in many areas they are also similar. Without getting to deep I assure that once a woman owns her confidence, leadership, and sexual energy she begins to stand in self-assurance. A woman who knows her confidence, who doesn't seek approval nor accolades, yet moves in humble silence is a vessel force truly to be reckoned with. Why, would she be a force? How did she become such a force?

Remember this chapter is about your strength and your truth. Now why would that particular woman be a force? At some point let me assure you that this 'Alpha Woman' stopped living towards and for others expectations. Rather people did or didn't walk with her, she learned how to no longer allow individuals to disturb her state of mind, energy, atmosphere, vibration, and most of all her peace. She actually learned how to selfishly love herself. She learned how not to engage in unproductive conversations, know when anyone is attempting to bait her, and how to leave any room when she is finished. Her strength enables her to walk into any atmosphere with her head up and walk out of any room embodied by her truth. This woman have learned how not to say no to the God inside and outside of her when her conditions and situations get and have gotten tough and sometimes very intense to bear. Yet she made it! Her yes remained yes in spite of the obstacle. She understands that she was sign, sealed, and approved by the greater power so she seeks no same level power approval. Experience, assurance, grace, and mercy has her every step of the way. When she begins to live in more than a conqueror as our ancestors, she relies on the roots and not the stories.

Ready Or Not It's Me

There are many traveled roads that assist women to arrive to destination SELF-ASSURANCE. She becomes a force by being her best cheerleader, inputting positive affirmations on a daily basis until it becomes her life, and having a healthy balance and understanding that we are all striving and dehumanizing anyone is actually that individual hating on herself. Take time and revisit your Potted Plant and see how you can implement your negative foundation for positive restructuring. Make no mistake about it, if you don't start today, time is wasting for change. You may be the first one in your family to break the unhealthy foundation.

Ready Or Not It's Me

Self-Reflectatory Time:

Name 5 Strengths:

a) _____

b) _____

c) _____

d) _____

e) _____

What are 5 Truths:

a) _____

b) _____

c) _____

d) _____

e) _____

Ready Or Not It's Me

Specify 5 Things That You Love:

    a) _____

    b) _____

    c) _____

    d) _____

    e) _____

Specify 5 Things That You Will Not Compromise:

    a) _____

    b) _____

    c) _____

    d) _____

    e) _____

Specify 5 Negative Things That You Want to Change to Be More Positive for your Family:

    a) _____

    b) _____

    c) _____

    d) _____

    e) _____

Knowing, mastering, and balancing self by not allowing the expectations of others to infiltrate your mind builds your foundation and self-confidence.

Selfless Love

WOMAN. WOUNDED. WARRIOR.

YOU CAN'T FIT MY SHOES

Something's are unexpected while others are planned

You Can't Fit My Shoes
8.

    We all have stories and our stories are important. We must decide on what side we choose to develop, the victim side or victor. I mentioned this V & V earlier. Many of us have mentally allowed ourselves to stay on the side as victims. Depending on who we conversate with we decide what V to carry our energy. Can you imagine if Harriett Tubman remained in the mindset and energy of victim? What about Sojourner Truth? What about Barbara Jordan? Think about Ruby Bridges and Lyda D. Newman. These women all have stories, yet they didn't settle for victim they all decided to rise above their conditions and their situations. I image that these women often moved in silence. I image that they cried at night and woke up with a game plan. They didn't have time to get so tied up in their emotions due to them understanding their purpose.

    Before identifying with any other hat that I wear throughout the year I identify as woman, female. We as females are very important. If I was to compare female in the animal kingdom many would understand that as lioness we hunt and feed the pride. As eagles the female establish territory and build the nest as they take care of the nestlings. As bears the female is a full-time care giver and teaches the cubs how to keep the den in their early months. As female elephants they stand as the matriarch. In one way or another we as females stand in intricate roles as did our ancestors. There are many times when we must make a decision from survival mode to get to the next level of our lives, especially with children. We may never know exactly as to why we made the decision at that time, we just know that it was the best one that we could think of during that particular season.

You Can't Fit My Shoes

We take a lot of shit from those around us yet at some point we honestly have to put our foot down and remind everyone in our circle that you will not allow anyone, mother, man, child, friends or self to devalue you as a human being on any level. This is how you'll know when you are ready to stand up and advocate and protect yourself at all cost. When a women have been wounded enough she will get tired of being tired and set some real healthy boundaries across the board of her life or die trying. If I put my foot down and set boundaries for my children I most definitely will have boundaries set for any man who desire to be in my life. These boundaries are for rather we are sexual involved or not.

Here is a note for the young female who loves to say "I'm grown," yet still needs mom for more than half of her living! At some point I desire for my daughters to hear me as not just mom yet as big sister. Now listen, if my child is depending on me to provide room, board, clothing, and medical then I am still seated and moving as mommy. When my children have children and they can begin to understand some of my wounds and uncertain movement and reasoning then I choose to no longer be mommy, I am mom because they have now taken the position of mommy. I have to teach my children and unrelentlessly encourage them to get out there and get it, whatever it takes to push through and get it for her and her children, while I still have breathe and I can assist and navigate with common sense and direction. I always desire for my children, my Queens, to be better than me.

You Can't Fit My Shoes

I have walked and pursued life with children as M.O.M. (manager over most), because God is ruler of all! I don't need to put down the man that left or need the pat on my back for doing what I was designed to do, which is nurture my babies to health through my growth, gaining my identity, and personal storms. Remember we all have stories even that man that you choose not to let go of or the man that you will not allow your children to see though he is a great father, yet you are no longer together. Aye Sis, give him his penis, his issues, his clothes, and his car back or keep yours. Now, lift up your head, stop looking for someone to come and pat you on your back and be a better you because you can!

Our ancestors fought because they desired for us to have better situations then they did. They desired for us to have what they couldn't have for themselves. They couldn't do this by giving into the societal ideas. They did this by never forgetting our roots. We are not required to understand everything that we are going through and I emphasis the words, "going through." Yet we still have purpose to fulfill and battles to overcome. Many of our struggles, mental barriers and turbulences are because we attempt to figure out what we are going through and why we are going through it. In many seasons you have to learn how to just embrace and hold on. Learning how to embrace our seasons as our forefathers and mothers did allows us to get through circumstances that we sometimes have gotten ourselves into, or the test that prepares us for the next level, and through all seasonal periods of our lives.

You Can't Fit My Shoes

Most of us are warriors yet when ones self-esteem or mental being has been tampered with it is most difficult to see the trees through the forest. Here are a few tips to assist in your new direction.

1. Ladies we must develop mental toughness. Developing mental toughness doesn't leave us so vulnerable to so many of the emotional turbulences that can often throw us off.

2. The Potted Plant Method is a tool to assist us with visualizing our success by seeing what causes our dysfunctional behavior patterns and reactions. When we learn how to respond, which means that we think the situation through, oppose to reacting then we can overcome our attitudes and mental turmoil's. Our different seasons prepare and equip us.

3. Ladies control your sexual energy. I didn't get into a deep enough conversation in regard to the clitorises part of us that drives us which is why we at times sleep with the same man over and over knowing that he isn't on our energy wave. Our bodies be calling for him. That part of the woman that we truly don't acknowledge nor talk about on a regular larger scale. Basically, ladies control your throb.

4. Be humility. I truly know that if God wasn't the captain of my ship, I would have crashed without ever leaving the port again. I know why something's were never able to touch or destroy me.

You Can't Fit My Shoes

5. Get to know people for yourself. Sometimes we occupy in similar circles and find ourselves disliking or questioning individuals because someone in the circle had a few choose words about the individual. Set your own rule of thumb and examine people for yourself.

6. Learn Men – there are two definite that I learned about men from an older gentleman.

A) That when men put their hands in their pockets they go nuts. It's a man natural thang!

B) That when a man is interested, he will show his interest.

Please stop getting upset because of your expectations of a man. He does things simple, tunneled, and focused. He is not the multitasker. There are many more suggestions that I can make yet I prefer to offer little chucks and meditate on my movement. At the beginning and end of the day I must be happy with me. Anyone who steps into my life should only be able to make happier not make me happy. My choices, my decisions, my yes, and my no's must make sense and assure that I have peace of mind. I wrote this book because I have sealed my life and allowed these principles and suggestions to mature me since becoming a young mother at the age of fifteen. Did you know that after COVID nearly one out of five people were diagnosed with mental health?

I believe that each one of us have some type of mental discourse and emotional turbulence nevertheless applying this book to your life is a mental changer!

Grassrooted Queendom

THE TRANSFORMATION AND THE HEALING

EMOTIONAL INTELLIGENCE

Something's are unexpected while others are planned

Emotional Intelligence

9.

My dear brothers and sisters,

You may still be in the dark as to what Emotional Intelligence is and how do you figure out your own Emotional Intelligence. Look I stated before that this book has nothing to do with my boasting and popping my collar. I earnestly need you to step outside of your mental box and close your eyes if need be, to hear me.

Now, what is Emotional Intelligence? Emotional Intelligence (EI) refers to a person's ability to recognize, understand, and manage their own emotions, as well as to perceive and influence the emotions of others. Many of us as a people are not there due to so many reasons so I cannot just pinpoint one. Yet, let me ask you this:

If a friend or just a person you know had an opportunity to go to another level of success, would you?
a)   Immediately get upset.
b)   Try to talk them out of the opportunity.
c)   Be genuinely happy for them.

Not being able to celebrate others is one of those topics that we can speak on and on and on about.

With this example, today, I want to speak to you about a very important aspect of our lives, one that can have a profound impact on our relationships, our work, and our overall well-being. I'm talking about emotional intelligence. E.I. explained again:

Emotional Intelligence

    Emotional intelligence is the ability to identify, understand, and manage our own emotions and the emotions of those around us. It's about being aware of our feelings, being able to express them in a constructive way, and being able to empathize with others. And it's something that can truly transform our lives for the better.

    Firstly, emotional intelligence can improve our relationships. When we are emotionally intelligent, we are better able to understand the needs and feelings of those around us. We can communicate more effectively, resolve conflicts more easily, and build stronger, more meaningful connections with others. We can also be more supportive and understanding when someone is going through a tough time, and we can offer comfort and encouragement when they need it most.

    Secondly, emotional intelligence can enhance our work and career. When we are emotionally intelligent, we are better able to manage stress, stay motivated, and work collaboratively with others. We can also be more effective leaders, able to inspire and motivate our teams to achieve great things. And we can be more creative, able to come up with innovative solutions to complex problems.

Emotional Intelligence

    Lastly, emotional intelligence can benefit our own well-being. When we are emotionally intelligent, we are better able to manage our own emotions, which can help us to feel more in control of our lives. We can also be more resilient, able to bounce back from setbacks and difficulties with greater ease. And we can be more compassionate and kinder, which can bring a sense of purpose and fulfillment to our lives.

    So, my dear brothers and sisters, I urge you to cultivate your emotional intelligence. Take the time to understand your own emotions, and practice expressing them in a constructive way. Take the time to listen to others and try to understand their feelings and perspectives. And take the time to be kind and compassionate, both to yourself and to those around you.

    By doing so, you will not only improve your own life, but you will also contribute to a world that is more understanding, more empathetic, and more peaceful. Let us all strive to be more emotionally intelligent and let us work together to build a better future for ourselves and for generations to come.

    Thank you, and may God bless you all.

Unforgettable Plays

APPLICABLE HABITS

Learn about applying transformational tools in the next book *The Art of Positive Thinking*. In The Art of Positive Thinking, you'll have a review of The Art of Remaining and then more tools to use and apply to your life.

To invite Samella England to speak at your next event you can send an old fashion post letter to: **7918 El Cajon Blvd #N355, La Mesa CA, 91942** or email ***artofremaining@gmail.com***. Please include the event topic, population, and your entity type. Include the "Speaker Request" from the next page.

LEARN MORE @

www.OneCommunityNetwork.org

Samella England Speaker's Request:

Organization's Information: _____

Client's Name or
Business Name: _____

Address:
(City, State, ZIP Code): _____

Phone number: _____

Email Address: _____

Event Topic: _____

Name and address of event venue: _____

Contact person of event, name, title, phone, email:
_____

Anticipated number of attendees: _____

Date of Event:_____ Start time:_____ End time: _____

Schedule of intermissions, if any: _____

TAKE SOME YOU TIME
It's All About You Boo!

- Be Mindful of the present!
- Discover the true you through prayer and meditation!
- SELF CARE ISN'T SELFISH
- Tap into the endurance of our ancestors victories!
- Think Positive! Feel Positive! Be Positive! And Breathe...

Through the search of finding you, you'll experience many different turbulences. The photos above provide some suggestions to use to relax, breathe, and explore. Light a candle, sage, or santo wood to enjoy the smell and cleanse the air, your thoughts and align yourself through prayer or meditation. And never forget the Word of God, B.I.B.L.E.

JOIN 14 - DAY
Yang Challenge

1) Make you a positive music list of about 10 to 14 songs
2) Pick 5 songs to listen to the first 5 days
3) Every morning look in the mirror and state positive affirmations about you.
4) Get your stickies and stick them around your mirror so that it's not out of sight
5) Only speak positive words to yourself and to others
6) If you feel anything but safe leave the atmosphere and rebalance with your positive music
7) Repeat the first steps for the second week and listen to your next 5 positive songs

To accept this Yang Challenge, join Loved B2L and obtain more Inspiration by going to www.OneCommunityNetwork.com.

SIGNUP NOW

JOIN 7-DAY
Yang Challenge

For 7 days you are only allowed to speak Positive Affirmations, Manifestations, Celebrations for you and others who are around you. There is always a light in the midst of the struggle. Your challenge is to only speak to the best outcome for each circumstance that comes against you this week. Believing and knowing that what and whoever is coming up against you is temporary and that the best will only happen for you with the correct response after the initial reaction. To accept this Yang Challenge, join Loved B2L and obtain more Inspiration by going to www,OneCommunityNetwork.com.

SIGNUP NOW

MY PLAYLIST SAMPLE
Yang Challenge

Just In Case You Need A Start

Arrested Development – People Everyday
Des'ree – You Gotta Be
Angie Stone – Brotha
Erykah Badu – Tyrone
Mary Mary – Walking
Tamela Mann – Change Me
Tasha Cobbs Leonard & Kierra Sheard – Your Spirit
Jessica Reedy – Something Out of Nothing
Charles Jenkins – Awesome (Remix)
Koryn Hawthorne – Won't He Do It
India Arie – Steady Love

SIGNUP NOW

POETRY CORNER

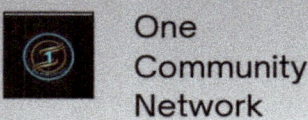
One Community Network

The Truth Is That Your Tomorrow Begins Today:

The Truth About Tomorrow,
It Begins Today

The truth about tomorrow is that it truly begins today. Our actions, our loyalty, our treatment or mistreatment of others, yes even the things that we say. The development of our brains beginned before our birth. So again, I say our actions, our loyalties, our treatment and mistreatment of others, yes even the things that we say beginned before we met Mother Earth. Now chooses is a n opportunity that was introduced to you and me. Yet misleading persuasive options is the road often traveled you see. "If it feels good then do it" I hear the society say. "No matter how many are killed or hurt, just do it, you may!" Yet the truth about tomorrow, it begins today. Today the present where we can add positive value to our tomorrow. We can lift hung down heads, give a smile to a stranger, give food to the hungry, do our part at making this season a better place to help take away someone else's sorrow.

One Community Network

Reaching, stretching your hands and heart out to a neighbor. Encouraging, empowering them to know that they are blessed and that they have favor. So you see how choices is a major part of each of our lives.

We can share, uplift, celebrate successes and push more than "just thrive!" That misleading persuasive optional road can be turned around. To enable every man, woman, and child to lift their eyes up to the sky away from the ground. In order to make tomorrow a better today we must remember that the truth about tomorrow most definitely begins today

WRITTEN BY
Samella England

You Are God's Design and You Can Manage Your Life With the Right Tool Applications

E.I.
NOTES

WHEN SETTING GOALS, MAKE SURE IT FOLLOWS YOUR EXPECTATIONAL STRUCTURE. USE THE QUESTION BELOW TO CREATE YOUR GOALS. 3 TO 5 AT A TIME TO REDUCE FRUSTRATIONS.

N — WHAT DO I WANT TO ACCOMPLISH?

O

T

E

S

E.I. NOTES

WHEN SETTING GOALS, MAKE SURE IT FOLLOWS YOUR EXPECTATIONAL STRUCTURE. USE THE QUESTION BELOW TO CREATE YOUR GOALS. 3 TO 5 AT A TIME TO REDUCE FRUSTRATIONS.

N — WHAT DO I WANT TO ACCOMPLISH?

O

T

E

S

E.I.
NOTES

WHEN SETTING GOALS, MAKE SURE IT FOLLOWS YOUR EXPECTATIONAL STRUCTURE. USE THE QUESTION BELOW TO CREATE YOUR GOALS. 3 TO 5 AT A TIME TO REDUCE FRUSTRATIONS.

N — WHAT DO I WANT TO ACCOMPLISH?

O

T

E

S

E.I. NOTES

WHEN SETTING GOALS, MAKE SURE IT FOLLOWS YOUR EXPECTATIONAL STRUCTURE. USE THE QUESTION BELOW TO CREATE YOUR GOALS. 3 TO 5 AT A TIME TO REDUCE FRUSTRATIONS.

N — WHAT DO I WANT TO ACCOMPLISH?

O

T

E

S

www.ingramcontent.com/pod-product-compliance
Lightning Source LLC
Chambersburg PA
CBHW042353070526
44585CB00028B/2916